QUILTING IN THE COUNTRY

PROJECTS AND RECIPES TO CELEBRATE LIFE'S SPECIAL MOMENTS

Jane Quinn

Martingale®
& COMPANY

CONTENTS

Introduction 7

Welcome Baby Sweet Pea 8

    Ruffles and Bows for Sweet Pea 10

    Welcome Baby Sweet Pea Recipes 14

    Clever Baby-Shower Ideas 15

    Welcome to the Neighborhood 16

An Invitation to Tea 21

    Circle of Friends 22

    An Invitation to Tea Recipes 25

    YaYa's Yo-Yos 26

    Posy Tea Cozy and Drip Catcher 28

    English Teapot Pad 34

For the Pair 36

    A Toast to the Special Pair 38

    Words of Wisdom 42

    For the Pair Recipes 47

Autumn Harvest 48

   Leaves from a Fall Walk 50

   Ring of Leaves in Their Shouting Colors 54

   Autumn Harvest Recipe 59

   A Glorious Trip 60

Sweet Sugar Cookie Memories 65

   Grandma's Memories 66

   Cute as a Bug Tree Ornaments 70

   Hosting a Cookie Exchange 75

   Cookie Exchange Recipes 75

Prairie Tablecloth Tree Skirt 77

Warm Up with Winter Friends 80

   Wool Mitten Friends 82

   Tips for a Fun-Filled Winter Picnic 85

   No Strings Attached 86

   Warm Up with Winter Friends Recipe 89

Quiltmaking Basics 90

Resources 96

About the Author 96

INTRODUCTION

*D*ear Friends,

Please let me open my home to you and share some of my entertaining and quilting ideas. We all know that happy memories with friends reinforce the positive things in life. The benefit of maintaining friendships is a top priority for me, and I intend to nurture your spirit and imagination. Together we can create some memories that will last a lifetime. This is a gift we give to ourselves.

My intent is to live simply and fully, truly relishing each moment. But life isn't simple, is it? In many ways we have worked hard for this rich and complicated lifestyle. True, life is demanding and the family, friends, work, and home that I love all require my attention. However, it is also important to connect with people we care about and spend time talking and laughing. It is necessary to be generous with our time and talents. In very simple ways, we can spread thoughtfulness and kindness in good times and not-so-good times. Sometimes a get-together can be sweet and sad, other times glorious and giddy.

I won't entertain if it becomes an attempt to merely get through the trials and tasks of the day. I want to notice all the details. Entertaining is an extension of my creative self and an expression of my spirit. It satisfies my soul. Sharing a meal means sharing myself. I want to decorate the table in my ever-favorite colors. I want to walk into the room and see something beautiful. The environment must be relaxed, comfortable, and free from formality. My style of entertaining is much like my approach to patchwork: simple, accessible, and—hopefully—refreshing.

Creativity isn't restricted to any one form; it can be embodied in cooking, quilting, or conversation, among other things. What is really fun for me is having time to think, dream, and contemplate the menu and a cleverly decorated table. Of course I want to strike the right balance without too much effort. I don't have a lot of time, but I love getting out some unexpected nostalgic treasures for the table—my sheep collection or a rustic red barn with a metal roof (and a miniature quilt hung on one end, of course!). I have an antique cast-iron John Deere tractor that looks fun on a table, or I'll add jars full of buttons, old wooden spools of thread, pretty little appliqué scissors, and other vintage sewing notions, too. At one party my theme was "Days of Wine and Roses." My small antique glass bottles held a rose at each place setting.

The truth is that entertaining is about a lot more than the food we eat. Of course, creating an interesting menu is important, but truly taking time to pause and reflect on this intimate celebration of life is what really matters. After a recent party, I felt such happiness at being able to spend time with friends. I was joyful as I hand washed and dried my mother's old goblets while thinking of the blessing of special times with friends and family. We are blessed! Life is good!

Jane

WELCOME BABY SWEET PEA

We recently received an email from a friend who announced that she and her husband are in the process of adopting a baby girl from China. The couple has two young boys, and a little girl would be the perfect addition to their family. Our friend asked if we would serve as references for the adoption process. Of course, my husband, Bill, and I were thrilled to put in a good word.

Interestingly, on the day I was preparing to complete the adoption form for our friends, an email came from another close friend telling me

8

that her mother had died. Her mother was a peaceful, quiet, and gentle soul. As happens so many times, a special person leaves our lives at the same time that a new member comes into the circle. The passages in our lives teach us so much. We all find wisdom in our experiences and then weave it into our own rich tapestry of existence, finding comfort in the community of people who join us on our life journey.

But what about a gathering to mark this milestone and the adoption of this baby girl?

At a special party, neighbors, friends, and family can offer blessings, advice, and stories about raising their own children. And here's an exercise to demonstrate interconnectedness. The guests pass a skein of yarn from one to another, tying the yarn around his or her wrist before passing it on. Upon completing the circle, the yarn is cut and each person has a yarn bracelet. What a wonderful symbol of the importance of this new addition to the circle.

Ruffles and Bows
FOR SWEET PEA

CREATED BY JANE QUINN. QUILTED BY BEV PALM.

*I*N OUR COMMUNITY OUTSIDE BOZEMAN, MONTANA, THE ANNUAL
SWEET PEA FESTIVAL IS HELD ON THE FIRST WEEKEND OF AUGUST.
SWEET PEA IS AN ARTS-AND-CRAFTS EXTRAVAGANZA THAT DRAWS MANY TO
THE COMMUNITY FOR CLASS REUNIONS, WEDDINGS, AND EVEN A FEW BABY
SHOWERS. SINCE "SWEET PEA" IS ALSO A COMMON TERM OF ENDEARMENT, THIS
QUILT WILL MAKE A PERFECT WALL QUILT FOR A BABY'S NURSERY.

GEORGIA BONESTEEL TAUGHT ME TO MAKE THESE THREE-DIMENSIONAL
BOW TIES. SHE SAID THE WOMAN WHO SHARED THE TECHNIQUE WITH HER
TOLD HER TO SHARE IT WITH AS MANY QUILTERS AS SHE COULD. NOW I'M
SHARING IT WITH YOU!

QUILT SIZE: 46½" x 52½" • BLOCK SIZE: 4" x 4"

MATERIALS

Yardage is based on 42"-wide fabric.

1⅓ yards of green print for sashing and outer border

¾ yard of yellow print for gathered border

⅛ yard *each* of 10 prints for bow ties

⅛ yard *each* of 5 prints for bow-tie backgrounds

1 sweet pea poster print*, at least 18½" x 24½"

½ yard of fabric for binding

3¼ yards of fabric for backing

53" x 59" piece of batting

*See "Resources" on page 96 for ordering information.

CUTTING

All measurements include ¼"-wide seam allowances.

From *each* of the 10 bow-tie prints, cut:
9 squares, 2½" x 2½" (90 total)

From *each* of the 5 bow-tie background prints, cut:
12 squares, 2½" x 2½" (60 total)

From the green print, cut:
3 strips, 1½" x 40"
28 pieces, 2½" x 4½"
11 strips, 2½" x 40"

From the yellow print, cut:
9 strips, 2½" x 40"

From the binding fabric, cut:
6 strips, 2½" x 40"

MAKING THE BOW-TIE BLOCKS

For each Bow-Tie block, choose a bow-tie color and
a bow-tie background print, mixing the combina-
tions for interest. For each block you will need three
2½" x 2½" squares of a bow-tie print and two 2½" x
2½" squares of a background.

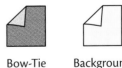

Bow-Tie
block fabric

Background
fabric

1. Fold one bow-tie print square in half with wrong
    sides together to make a 1¼" x 2½" rectangle.

2. Sandwich the rectangle between one bow-tie print square and one background square, with the right sides together and raw edges aligned. Stitch across one edge as shown, catching the short end of the rectangle in the seam. Unfold as shown.

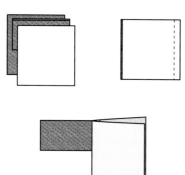

3. Sandwich the other end of the rectangle between the remaining bow-tie print and background squares. Stitch the edge, catching the short end of the rectangle in the seam as shown. Unfold to form a "bridge" between the two sides as shown.

4. Open the rectangle and refold, aligning all raw edges and seams as shown. Stitch the top edge.

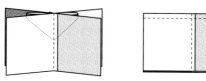

5. Lay the block out flat. It should measure 4½" x 4½".

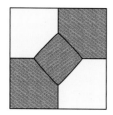

6. Repeat for a total of 30 Bow-Tie blocks.

PIECING THE QUILT

1. Trim the poster print, if necessary, to measure 18½" x 24½". Remove the stabilizer paper from the back of the poster print. Sew the three 1½" green print strips together end to end. Cut two strips, 1½" x 24½", and sew them to the top and bottom edges of the poster print. Cut two strips, 1½" x 20½", and sew them to the sides of the poster print.

2. Lay out the blocks around the center sweet pea panel to decide placement. Form the horizontal rows by alternating six Bow-Tie blocks with five of the 2½" x 4½" green print rectangles. Be sure to orient the Bow-Tie blocks in the same direction. Stitch the pieces together. Press toward the green print rectangles. Repeat to make a total of four rows.

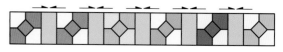

Make 4.

3. For the side sections, alternate three Bow-Tie blocks with four of the 2½" x 4½" rectangles of green print. Be sure to orient the Bow-Tie blocks in the same direction as in the horizontal Bow-Tie block rows. Stitch the pieces together and press toward the rectangles. Make two vertical rows, one for each side of the center poster section.

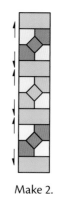

Make 2.

4. Sew the eleven 2½" strips of green print together end to end. Cut four strips, 2½" x 34½", and sew one strip to the top of two of the horizontal Bow-Tie block rows made in step 2. Stitch the two row units together as shown

to make the top section of the quilt. Repeat for the bottom section of the quilt, sewing the 2½" strips to the bottom of each Bow-Tie block row.

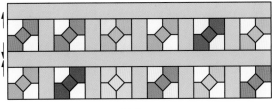

Make 1.

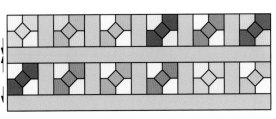

Make 1.

5. Stitch the side sections to the left and right sides of the poster section. Press toward the center. Join the three completed Bow-Tie block sections and press.

6. Cut two strips, 2½" x 44½", from the remaining long strip of green print. Sew to the right and left sides of the completed Bow-Tie block section.

ADDING BORDERS

1. Sew the 2½" strips of yellow print together end to end. Cut two strips, 2½" x 76", for the top and bottom borders. Sew two basting lines along both lengthwise edges of each strip, one at a scant ¼" and the other ⅛" closer to the edge. Gently pull the threads from the right side, gathering each strip until it measures 2½" x 38½". Pinning as needed, sew the gathered strips to the top and bottom of the quilt.

2. Cut two strips, 2½" x 96", from the yellow print for the side borders. Repeat the basting and gathering process until the strips measure 2½" x 48½". Pin and sew the gathered strips to the sides of the quilt.

Easy Marking

When pinning the gathered border, I use a corsage pin to mark the center. This distinguishes it from the other pins and I know immediately where the center is.

3. Cut two strips, 2½" x 42½", from the remaining long strip of green print pieced earlier. Sew to the top and bottom of the quilt. Cut two strips, 2½" x 52½", from the green print. Sew to the sides of the quilt.

FINISHING

1. Refer to "Layering and Basting" on page 93 to prepare your quilt for quilting.

2. Quilt by hand or machine as desired.

3. Bind the quilt using the 2½" strips, referring to "Binding" on page 94.

WELCOME BABY SWEET PEA RECIPES

A baby shower luncheon menu might include strawberries with balsamic vinegar, pasta salad, and chocolate mousse for dessert. Or, for something really different, ask guests to bring a box lunch to swap. This creates a unique way to mix and get acquainted at a baby shower. We did this at one shower I attended; the variety of choices was amazing. It was very enjoyable and everyone seemed pleased. The hostess provided a decadent dessert to top off the fun.

Strawberries with Balsamic Vinegar

INGREDIENTS

4 cups strawberries, washed, hulled, and quartered

3 tablespoons balsamic vinegar

3 tablespoons sugar

PREPARATION

1. Combine all ingredients and marinate for 30 minutes to 4 hours.

2. Sprinkle with freshly ground pepper immediately before serving.

Yield: 6 servings

Luncheon Turkey Salad

INGREDIENTS
Salad:

2½ pounds turkey, cooked and diced

1 can (20 ounces) sliced water chestnuts, well drained

2 pounds seedless grapes, halved

2 cups sliced celery

1 can (20 ounces) pineapple chunks, well drained

1 to 2 cups sliced almonds, toasted

Dressing:

3 cups mayonnaise

½ tablespoon curry powder (more if desired)

2 tablespoons soy sauce

2 tablespoons lemon juice

PREPARATION
Mix dressing ingredients together and combine with salad ingredients the night before serving.

Yield: 24 servings

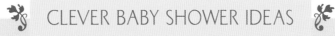
Baby quilts are the ones most frequently made for a special occasion—the baby's birth. Every newborn needs a special quilt to be wrapped up in. In addition to presenting a quilt, here are some unique ideas for making a baby shower a memorable event.

- Ask each guest to bring his or her baby photo. Guessing the identity of each person becomes a fun way to get acquainted. Also, if you can collect the photos in advance, frame them and use them at each place setting. The frame can be your gift to each guest.

- Have guests make a page for a baby book. The hostess provides an inspiring array of scrapbooking supplies, and each guest is free to embellish a page as desired. It's an interesting way for each person to contribute to a one-of-a-kind gift for the newborn.

- Send quilted postcard invitations. When my daughter and I hosted a baby shower, I used quilt labels to create a postcard invitation. A flannel cheater panel included printed quilt labels. Create the cards by sandwiching the quilt label, Timtex, and a piece of flannel; machine zigzag the three layers together. (There is also a fusible product, Fast2Fuse, that you can use in the center.) I used a permanent marker to address the invitation. The postal workers were happy to hand cancel the cards. Nonquilters were especially impressed with the invitation. (You may want to check with your local post office first. Busy locations may prefer that you put your invitations in envelopes.)

POSTCARD INVITATION BY JANE QUINN

Welcome
TO THE NEIGHBORHOOD

$\mathcal{T}$O SYMBOLIZE A WELCOME AND WILLINGNESS TO LEND A HELPING HAND, CONSIDER MAKING THIS FUN QUILT WITH HANDPRINTS OF THOSE WHO ARE WELCOMING A NEW ADDITION INTO THE FAMILY OR NEIGH-BORHOOD CIRCLE. PAINTED HANDPRINTS WERE PLACED LIKE WAVING FLOWERS IN A GARDEN ROW, AND THE NAMES WERE ADDED AS LEAVES. THE MOST IMPOR-TANT FEATURE IS TO ADD THE HANDPRINT OF THE NEW ADDITION WHEN HE OR SHE IS BIG ENOUGH. THIS NAP-SIZED QUILT IS PERFECT AS THE CHILD GROWS, AND IT WOULD ALSO BE APPROPRIATE FOR AN OLDER SIBLING.

QUILT SIZE: 44" x 75"

MATERIALS

Yardage is based on 42"-wide fabric.

2 yards of green fabric for grass and binding

1¾ yards of floral print for sashing and border

1⅛ yards of light blue fabric for sky

4½ yards of fabric for backing

50" x 81" piece of batting

1"-wide foam brushes

Assorted colors of fabric paint

Assorted green permanent fabric markers

Fresh Flowers

I always like to have a bouquet of fresh flowers when guests come. Place one in the powder room and your company will know that you gave extra care to prepare for their visit.

CUTTING

All measurements include ¼"-wide seam allowances.

From the floral print, cut:
1 piece, 35" x 40"
4 strips, 5" x 40"

From the green fabric, cut:
3 strips, 13" x 35", from the lengthwise grain
2½"-wide bias strips to total 250" in length

From the light blue fabric, cut:
1 piece, 35" x 40"

CUTTING THE CURVED PIECES

To make a pattern, enlarge the curve diagram on page 20 by 500%. Or, cut a piece of paper that is 10" x 35" and draw a curving line along one edge, using the diagram as a guide. Cut along the curved line. Each time you place the pattern on your fabric, you can rotate and/or flip the paper so that you get variety in your curves. Of course, you can add in your own variations, also.

CUTTING THE FLORAL PRINT

1. Place the pattern on the 35" x 40" piece of floral print fabric, with the long straight edge along the lengthwise raw edge of the fabric. Mark the edge of the curve on the fabric, and then cut along that line; set aside the piece you just cut off.

2. Rotate the pattern and place it on the remaining fabric, with the long straight edge of the pattern along the other straight lengthwise raw edge. Mark the edge of the curve and cut. Set aside the piece you just cut.

3. Cut a straight line lengthwise down the middle of the remaining fabric with two lengthwise curved edges. Now you have four pieces, each with one straight long edge and one curved long edge.

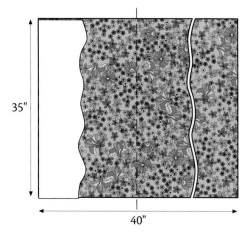

CUTTING THE LIGHT BLUE

1. Place the pattern on the 35" x 40" piece of light blue fabric so the curve is as close as possible to one lengthwise raw edge of the fabric. Mark the edge of the curve on the fabric and then cut along that line.

2. Rotate the pattern so that the curved edge runs lengthwise, parallel to the first cut, approximately one-third of the way across the width of the fabric. Mark the edge of the curve and cut. Set this piece aside.

3. Place the pattern on the fabric so that the curve is as close as possible to the remaining lengthwise raw edge. Mark the edge of the curve and cut along the line.

4. Place the pattern, rotating or flipping to create variety in the curves, so the curved edge runs lengthwise, parallel to the cut made in step 3, approximately halfway across the remaining piece of fabric. Mark the curve and cut. You now have three pieces with curved lengthwise edges on both sides.

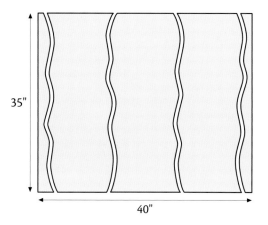

PREPARING THE BACKGROUND SECTIONS

Construct the center of the quilt in three sections, each with floral print on the bottom, green fabric in the middle, and blue fabric on top. I recommend waiting to sew the sections together until after the handprinting is complete, just in case of spilled paint or other accidents.

Note: Each time you are instructed to press under a curved edge, try to press ¼" or less to help keep your curves smooth.

1. Press under the curved edge of one of the floral print pieces. Place this piece on top of the bottom edge of a green piece so that the green piece extends 7" or 8" above the curved edge of the floral print piece. Make sure there is at least ½" of green extending below the curved edge of the floral print piece. Pin the area where the two fabrics overlap. Using a zigzag or decorative stitch, topstitch along the curve to join the pieces.

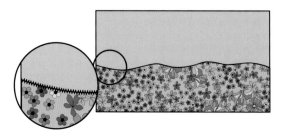

2. Press under the bottom curved edge of one of the light blue pieces. Place this piece on top of the green piece just added so that the green extends at least ½" underneath the light blue piece. Pin and topstitch as before.

3. Repeat steps 1 and 2 to make two more sections.

HANDPRINTS

Collect handprints from friends and family—all who will be welcoming the child to the neighborhood. Just save a place for the child's handprint when he or she arrives!

1. Use a 1" foam brush to apply the paint to the hands, both right and left. Use a variety of colors and place the handprints on the blue fabric of each quilt section with some overlapping on the green. The hands should resemble waving flowers. Refer to the diagram at right and the photograph on page 16 for placement guidelines.

2. Add stems and leaves using green permanent fabric markers, adding names along the stems or inside the leaves as desired. Follow the manufacturer's instructions on the paint and markers for setting the designs.

ASSEMBLING THE QUILT TOP

Once the paints are dry and the designs have been set, you are ready to join the three quilt sections.

1. Press under the curved edge of blue fabric along the top of the bottom quilt section. Place the straight edge of the floral print piece from the middle quilt section underneath the top curved edge of the first light blue piece so that the floral print extends at least ½" underneath the blue. Pin and topstitch as described in "Preparing the Background Sections."

2. Add the top quilt section, following the same steps.

3. Press under the curved edge of the blue fabric along the top quilt section. Place the straight edge of the fourth floral piece underneath the top curved edge of the third light blue piece so that the floral print extends at least ½"

underneath the blue. (Do not press under the curved edge of the fourth floral piece.) Pin and topstitch. Note that the top edge of your quilt has a curve.

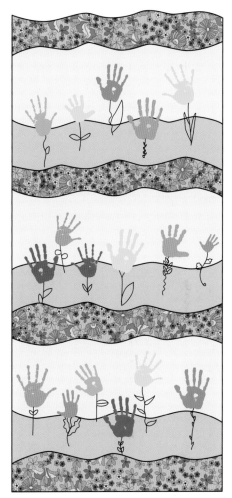

4. Trim the sides of the quilt, if necessary, to even up the edges of the various layers of floral, green, and blue fabrics. Sew two of the 5" x 40" strips of floral print together end to end. Sew to the side of the quilt, matching one end of the long strip with the bottom edge of the quilt. Let the extra length of the strip extend beyond the top of the quilt. Press the seam open, and then cut a continuation of the top curve into the border strip.

5. Repeat with the two remaining 5" x 40" floral strips to add a border to the other side of the quilt.

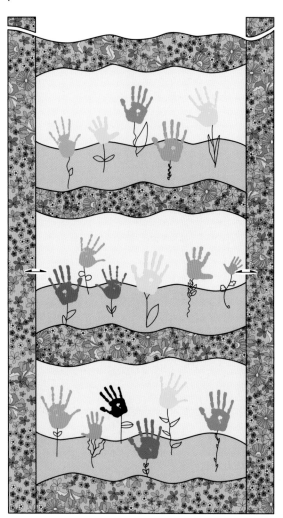

FINISHING

1. Refer to "Layering and Basting" on page 93 to prepare your quilt for quilting.

2. Quilt by hand or machine as desired.

3. Bind the quilt using the 2½" bias strips, referring to "Binding" on page 94. Pin and sew the binding on carefully so that it does not stretch along the three straight edges of the quilt.

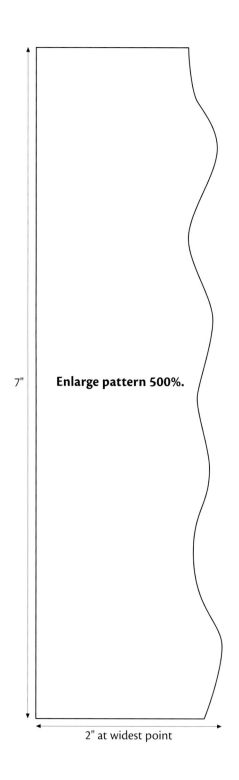

7"

Enlarge pattern 500%.

2" at widest point

AN INVITATION TO TEA

I consider my Lenox china to be among my most valuable possessions. The ivory-colored, silver-edged fluted china is very beautiful. I inherited the precious cups and saucers after my beloved grandmother Emma died.

Our family was large and when we went on vacation we would always bring a memento back to Grandmother, often a teacup and saucer. She always remembered who had given her what and would use the gifts whenever those family members were visiting for coffee.

Her cups and saucers were rather precariously displayed. If you hadn't visited for a while, your cup would be near the bottom and that would require quite a bit of careful shuffling, but I don't remember anything ever breaking. Our family didn't drink much tea, so we would have coffee with Grandmother instead.

On the other hand, our retired neighbor, Mrs. Fitzgerald, had a demitasse collection that she meticulously displayed on special racks built into her dining room walls. Our homes were very close together and we could see from our dining room into hers. When we baked, we would usually take a plate of goodies to her. That meant we would be invited in for tea. Even when our daughter, Anne, was a young child, she was allowed to choose which of the special cups she could use for the impromptu tea party.

When Mrs. Fitzgerald passed away, her daughter gave me a very lovely Blue Willow demitasse cup. When my granddaughter Quinn was about to celebrate her seventh birthday, I sent the demitasse cup and saucer to her, writing about her mother's relationship with Mrs. Fitzgerald. I now have lovely photographs of Quinn using the gift for the first time at her birthday tea party with seven of her girlfriends.

CIRCLE OF FRIENDS

CREATED BY KATHY CENTER AND SHARON ANDRIOLO

$\mathcal{L}$ AYER THIS CHARMING LITTLE TEATIME QUILT WITH HEIRLOOM LACE, A CROCHETED TABLECLOTH, OR ANTIQUE QUILTS. IT'S THE PERFECT SETTING FOR DISPLAYING YOUR FAMILY SILVER AND CHINA. THE DIRECTIONS ARE WRITTEN FOR EASY APPLIQUÉ, USING A PURCHASED INTER-FACING. NO CURVES TO SEW!

QUILT SIZE: 34" x 34" • BLOCK SIZE: 4" x 4"

MATERIALS

Yardage is based on 42"-wide fabric.

⅞ yard of large-scale floral theme print for blocks

¼ yard *each* of 3 green prints for blocks

¼ yard *each* of 3 pink prints for blocks

¼ yard *each* of 3 pale yellow prints for blocks

½ yard of yellow solid for binding

1⅓ yards of fabric for backing

40" x 40" piece of thin batting, such as Thermore or flannel

3 panels of Quiltsmart Drunkard's Path printed interfacing

CUTTING

All measurements include ¼"-wide seam allowances.

From *each* of the 3 pink prints, cut:
8 squares, 4½" x 4½" (24 total)

From *each* of the 3 pale yellow prints, cut:
4 squares, 4½" x 4½" (12 total)

From the large-scale floral print, cut:
44 squares, 4½" x 4½"

From *one* of the green prints, cut:
8 squares, 4½" x 4½"

From *each* of the remaining 2 green prints, cut:
4 squares, 4½" x 4½" (8 total)

From the yellow solid, cut:
5 strips, 2" x 40"

INSTRUCTIONS

Using the Quiltsmart printed interfacing is a breeze. Each 4½" square of Quiltsmart will go with one 4½" square of fabric to create two appliqué pieces: an arc and a quarter circle. The appliqué pieces can then be fused onto background squares according to the color arrangement desired and stitched by machine. Note that you will have extra arc pieces that you can use in another project.

1. Cut the Quiltsmart interfacing into 36 squares along the dashed lines. Place one 4½" print square on one Quiltsmart square with the right side of the fabric against the bumpy side of the interfacing. Do not fuse!

2. Sew on the two *solid lines* of the curve that is printed on the interfacing. Cut on the dashed line between the two curves.

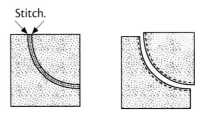

Stitch.

3. Turn right side out and finger-press. Do not use an iron! You will have one arc and one quarter circle. These are the appliqué pieces that will be fused to the backgrounds.

4. Repeat steps 1 through 3 using all 24 of the 4½" pink print squares and all 12 of the 4½" pale yellow print squares. Set aside 8 pink appliqué arcs and 4 pale yellow appliqué arcs; they are extra and can be saved for a future project. You should now have 24 pink quarter circles, 16 pink arcs, 12 pale yellow quarter circles, and 8 pale yellow appliqué arcs.

5. Pair each appliqué piece with a green print or large-scale floral background fabric according to the diagrams below. Place the appliqué piece (A) with the fabric side up on the right side of the background square (B), lining up the outer edges. Fuse in place.

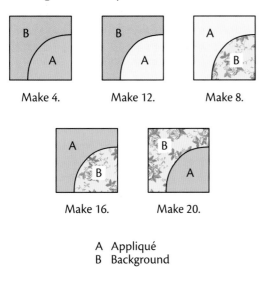

Make 4. Make 12. Make 8.

Make 16. Make 20.

A Appliqué
B Background

6. Using invisible thread, zigzag stitch along the curved edge of the appliqué piece to hold it in place.

7. Arrange the blocks in diagonal rows as shown in the quilt diagram. Sew together into rows, pressing the seams in the opposite direction from row to row. Sew the rows together and press.

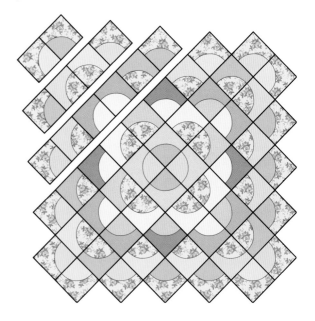

FINISHING

1. Refer to "Layering and Basting" on page 93 to prepare your quilt for quilting. The flannel or lightweight batting will make this a delightful summer-weight table quilt.

2. Quilt by hand or machine as desired.

3. Bind the quilt using the 2" strips, referring to "Binding" on page 94. The binding will present a bit of a challenge because of the inside corners. When sewing the binding onto the quilt, pull the edge of the quilt open as straight as possible when you approach an inside corner.

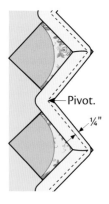

Pivot.

¼"

"There is no trouble so great or grave that cannot be much diminished by a nice cup of tea." — Bernard-Paul Heroux

Pavlova

A pavlova is a meringue shell topped with whipped cream and fruit. You will receive rave reviews when you serve this simple and sensational dessert on a footed cake plate.

INGREDIENTS

4 egg whites

Pinch of cream of tartar

8 rounded tablespoons sugar

2 teaspoons cornstarch

1 teaspoon vanilla

1 teaspoon vinegar

PREPARATION

1. Preheat the oven to 325°.

2. Beat egg whites with cream of tartar until stiff, but do not overbeat.

3. Add 4 rounded tablespoons sugar and beat until very stiff. Beat in the remaining 4 rounded tablespoons of sugar and cornstarch. Rub a little of the meringue between your fingers to feel if all sugar is dissolved.

4. Beat in vanilla and vinegar quickly.

5. Place on the shiny side of lightly buttered foil or a Silpat. Spread out to form a circle about 6" to 8" in diameter. Allow space for the mixture to spread out while baking.

6. Place on the middle shelf in the oven, reset the oven to 200°, and bake for 1 to 1½ hours. After baking, leave the meringue shell on its tray in the oven, with the door ajar, until cold.

Ideally, the meringue shell should be rather cream-colored, not brown. It should be slightly sunken in the center, crisp on the outside, and have a marshmallow center.

When cool, carefully remove the meringue shell from the baking sheet, place onto a footed cake plate, and decorate with whipped cream and fresh fruit. Serve immediately.

The meringue shell can be made days before and kept in an airtight container. Other serving options are chocolate shavings instead of fruit, chocolate whipped cream with toasted almonds, or peppermint chocolate.

Peach Honey

This yummy recipe came from an old publication, the October 1928 issue of *Farm Life*.

PREPARATION

Peel 12 peaches that are not too ripe; remove the pits and put the peaches through a meat grinder or food processor. Add one whole orange, putting it through the grinder or processor. Use a cup of sugar to each cup of fruit and boil 20 minutes. Pour into jars and seal, turning upside down until cool, or put into containers and freeze.

Yaya's Yo-Yos

CREATED BY KATHY CENTER

*I*N SPAIN AND GREECE, GRANDMOTHERS ARE CALLED YAYA. I NAMED THIS LITTLE PROJECT FOR A SPECIAL FRIEND, WHOSE GRAND-CHILDREN CALL HER YAYA. YO-YOS ARE ALWAYS GREAT FUN TO MAKE AND PROVIDE A PERFECT CARRY-ALONG PROJECT. THIS IS ALSO A SPLENDID WAY TO USE SOME OF THOSE BUTTONS THAT WE ALL SAVE.

DOILY SIZE: 13" x 14"

MATERIALS

19 assorted 6" squares of fabrics for yo-yos

18 assorted buttons

Circle template, 6" or less in diameter*

Hand-quilting thread

Look in your cupboards for a plate or bowl of the right size to use for a template.

INSTRUCTIONS

1. Use the template to trace a circle on each 6" square of fabric. I like to draw on one square and then layer more squares underneath so that I can cut more than one at a time. Cut out all 19 circles. Fussy cut one circle, if desired, to use in the center.

2. Turn the edge of each circle under ¼" and sew ⅛" in from the fold, using basting stitches, all the way around the circle. You can use a double length of thread or quilting thread so the thread doesn't break. Pull the thread to gather the circle and create the yo-yo.

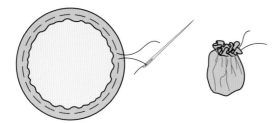

3. Make a knot in the basting thread and flatten the yo-yo. Repeat to make 19.

4. Set aside one yo-yo—the one that has the most pleasing print on the *ungathered* side. Sew a button onto the center of the gathered side of the other 18 yo-yos. This is an ideal time to use those wonderful buttons you've been collecting and didn't know what to do with.

5. Arrange the yo-yos as shown, turning over the one yo-yo without a button and placing it in the center. Using quilting thread, sew the yo-yos together with whipstitches where they touch.

Posy Tea Cozy
AND DRIP CATCHER

TEA COZY CREATED BY KATHY CENTER. DRIP CATCHER CREATED BY JULI ROGNLIE.

*I*T'S TIME FOR TEA. BREW UP A POT IN YOUR FAVORITE FLAVOR AND KEEP IT WARM AND COZY. LINGER AWHILE, PERHAPS ENJOYING A BOOK AS YOU SIP. THE LITTLE DRIP CATCHER WILL DELIGHT YOUR TEA PARTY GUESTS. JUST STORE IT ON THE TEAPOT SPOUT.

TEA COZY SIZE: 11" x 7" x 7"

MATERIALS FOR TEA COZY

Cotton yardage is based on 42"-wide fabric. Wool yardages are based on felted (washed and dried) wool that is at least 44" wide.*

½ yard of yellow print cotton for lining, flap, and binding

⅓ yard of pink wool for outside, handles, flap, and flower

¼ yard of green wool for handles, flap, and leaves

1 square, 6½" x 6½", of dark pink wool for flower

1 square, 6½" x 6½", of yellow wool for flower

1 button

5 sew-on snaps

*If your wool needs to be felted, purchase an extra 25%. However, some wool is commercially felted and does not need to be washed and dried.

FELTING WOOL

To felt wool, wash it in your washing machine with very hot water and a small amount of mild soap. The agitation of the machine helps in the felting process. Rinse with cold water and dry in a hot dryer. Remove from the dryer before completely dry. Smooth and lay the wool flat to dry completely. Most wool shrinks at least 20%. Working with felted wool is really fun and it does not fray.

CUTTING

All measurements include ¼"-wide seam allowances.

From the pink wool, cut:
1 piece, 7½" x 22½" (A)
2 pieces, 7½" x 7½" (B and C)
2 pieces, 1¼" x 12" (D)

From the yellow print cotton, cut:
1 piece, 7½" x 22½" (A)
2 pieces, 7½" x 7½" (B and C)
1 piece, 2½" x 4½" (G)
2 strips, 2" x 40"

From the green wool, cut:
1 piece, ½" x 4" (H)
2 pieces, ⅜" x 12" (F)

TEA COZY INSTRUCTIONS

1. Using the template E pattern on page 33, cut two E pieces from the ends of the 7½" x 22½" pink wool A piece as shown. Repeat with the 7½" x 22½" yellow print cotton A piece. (Snaps will be sewn on later. The wool E pieces will be used for the flap, but the yellow print E pieces can go in your scrap basket.)

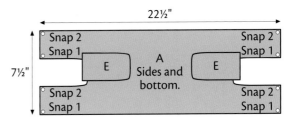

2. Insert the pink wool B piece (the front) and then the pink wool C piece (the back) into the long pink wool A piece (the sides and bottom) by stitching with right sides together, using a ¼" seam allowance. Repeat with the yellow print cotton A, B, and C pieces. This will create two separate tea cozy sections—the wool outer section and the cotton lining. Match them up, inserting the lining into the tea cozy, wrong sides together, and set aside.

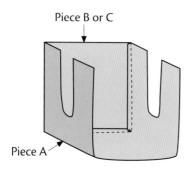

Piece B or C

Piece A

3. Make a flap for the tea cozy using the two pink wool E pieces that you cut from the ends of the pink wool A piece. Sew the two E pieces together along the three sides as shown, using a ¼" seam allowance and leaving the top open. Turn right side out and press.

4. Fold piece G, the 2½" x 4½" piece of yellow print cotton, in half lengthwise, wrong sides together. Zigzag stitch the raw edge of the long side. Open the piece with the seam in the back and press it flat. Turn the bottom raw edge under ¼" to the back and press.

5. Pin the ½" x 4" green wool H piece to the top of G. Sew H and G to the top of the flap made in step 3, using a zigzag stitch along the sides and bottom of the green wool H piece. The edges of G that stick out beyond the edges of H will be free. Sew a snap on the underside of the flap near the bottom edge. Pin the flap to the back center of the purse with right sides together and raw edges aligned.

6. Fold a 1¼" x 12" pink wool D piece (the handle) in half lengthwise and zigzag stitch the raw edge of the long side. Turn the zigzag to the top and place a ⅜" x 12" green wool F piece along the pink handle so that the green wool covers the line of zigzag stitching. Zigzag along the edges of the green. Repeat to make the second handle.

Make 2.

7. Pin the handles to the front and back of the outside of the tea cozy, right sides together and with raw edges matching. Each side of the handle should be about 2" from the center.

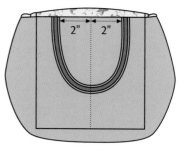

8. Sew the two 2" x 40" strips of yellow print cotton together end to end to make a binding. Refer to "Binding" on page 94. Think of the cotton lining as the backing of a quilt and the pink wool as the quilt top. Sew the binding to the entire raw edge of the tea cozy, catching the flap and handles on the top as you stitch. Turn the binding to the inside and stitch it by hand, mitering the corners.

9. Cut three flowers and two leaves from wool using the patterns on page 33. Zigzag the edges of each piece, if desired, which can have the effect of ruffling the edges. Hand sew in place on the front of the tea cozy. Add a button in the middle of the stacked flowers.

10. Sew a snap to the front of the tea cozy so that it lines up with the snap underneath the flap.

11. Refer to the diagram that accompanies step 1 on page 29 for placement, and sew snaps at each point so that the tea cozy will close together around the teapot.

TEA TRIVIA

The tea bag was invented in 1908 by a New York tea importer, Thomas Sullivan. He sent tea samples in little hand-sewn bags to his retail dealers and private customers. Sullivan was amazed to receive orders and surprised when people complained that the tea wasn't packaged in the little bags. His customers found the little bags convenient for brewing. As a result, gauze tea bags were substituted and the tea bag was born. Today, tea in specially treated paper bags accounts for 90% of the North American tea market.

MATERIALS FOR DRIP CATCHER

1" x 6" piece of green felted wool

1 flower button

10" length of 3mm silk ribbon

3" length of ⅛"-wide elastic

Needle and green thread

Hand-sewing needle with eye large enough for silk ribbon

Green RIT dye or green permanent felt-tip marker (optional)

CUTTING

From the green wool, cut a 1" x 3" rectangle. From the remainder of the green wool, cut two leaves using the pattern below.

Leaf
Cut 2.

DRIP CATCHER INSTRUCTIONS

1. If desired, dye the elastic green in a small bowl of hot water with a small amount of green RIT dye. The elastic will absorb the dye in just a few minutes. For an even quicker option, use a green permanent felt-tip marker to color the elastic. Let the elastic dry before continuing.

2. Thread your needle with green thread and knot one end. Place the 3" length of elastic, centered, across one end of the 1" x 3" piece of wool as shown. Beginning at the end of the wool with the elastic, roll the strip up tightly. The elastic will stick out on each side of the roll.

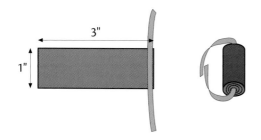

3. Holding the roll tightly, whipstitch along the raw edge to secure the roll. Bury the knot inside the roll.

4. Thread a needle with the 10" length of silk ribbon. Insert the needle down through one hole of the button (face up), through the top leaf, the two overlapped ends of elastic, and the bottom leaf. Layer the button, leaves, and elastic as shown as you secure them together with the silk ribbon. Bring the needle back up through the layers and tie the two ends of the ribbon snugly in a knot. Trim the ends of the ribbon.

BREWING THE PERFECT POT OF TEA

To orchestrate the perfect pot of tea, carefully fill the teakettle with cold water and bring it to a true boil. Warm your teapot with hot water, and then add the boiling water and the tea leaves. Let the tea leaves steep for exactly five minutes. The flavors will blossom. Strain the tea leaves or remove the tea bags.

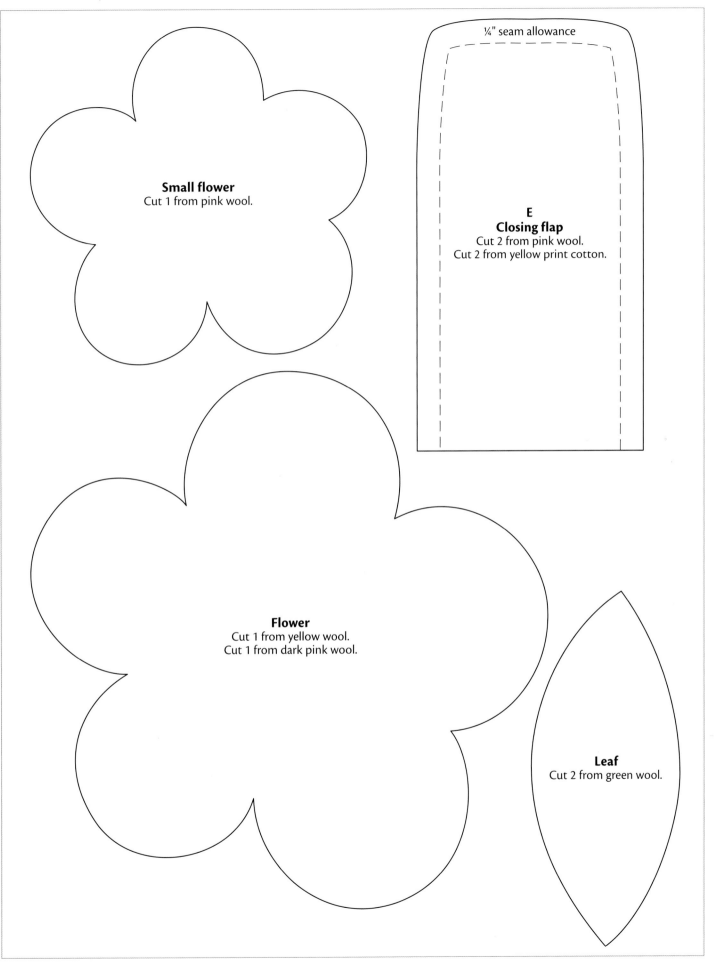

Small flower
Cut 1 from pink wool.

¼" seam allowance

**E
Closing flap**
Cut 2 from pink wool.
Cut 2 from yellow print cotton.

Flower
Cut 1 from yellow wool.
Cut 1 from dark pink wool.

Leaf
Cut 2 from green wool.

FOR THE PAIR

When we learned that our friends, the chef and the manager of a gourmet restaurant, were engaged to be married, we knew exactly what type of celebration we wanted to host for them. We decided that a wine-and-cheese pairing would be perfect.

Since we had attended and held wine-and-cheese tastings before, we knew just how to do it. We asked a friend with lots of knowledge about wine and cheese to introduce the pairings. We knew that his pairing parties were lots of fun, even for those who might not drink wine or care for smelly cheese—his sense of humor creates a fun atmosphere that is just right.

My husband and I, along with our host, decided that it would be fun if the pairings were presented in such a way that they weren't the obvious "perfect" pairing. Our host presented a variety of analogies regarding the balance needed in pairing wine and cheese, as well as in pairing couples. After each step in the pairing process, he asked the guests to vote for their favorite pair. It was a hilariously fun time.

A TOAST TO THE SPECIAL PAIR

$\mathcal{T}$RY MAKING THIS TABLE RUNNER IN CHAMPAGNE-COLORED FABRICS.
I MAKE RUNNERS TO FIT ACROSS THE BAR THAT SEPARATES MY
KITCHEN AND FAMILY ROOM. I PLACED THE GOBLETS AT THE ENDS SO THAT THE
MOTIFS ARE VISIBLE FROM BOTH SIDES WHEN HUNG OVER THE BAR.

TABLE RUNNER SIZE: 20¾" x 52"

MATERIALS

Yardage is based on 42"-wide fabric.

1⅓ yards of medium-scale print for outer border and binding

⅔ yard of large-scale print for center of runner

⅜ yard of purple print for goblets and inner border

⅛ yard of small-scale print for background of goblet blocks

1⅔ yards of fabric for backing

25" x 56" piece of batting

CUTTING

All measurements include ¼"-wide seam allowances.

From the purple print, cut:

2 squares, 4½" x 4½"

2 squares, 2" x 2"

4 squares, 1½" x 1½"

3 strips, 1½" x 40"

From the small-scale print, cut:

4 rectangles, 2½" x 4½"

8 squares, 2½" x 2½"

From the large-scale print, cut:

4 squares, 9" x 9"; cut in half diagonally once to make 8 triangles

1 rectangle, 11¾" x 20½"

From the medium-scale print, cut on the *lengthwise* grain:

2 strips, 4" x 43"

2 strips, 4" x 20¾"

4 strips, 2½" x 40"

INSTRUCTIONS

1. Mark diagonal lines from corner to corner on the wrong sides of the 1½" purple squares, the 2" purple squares, and the 2½" small-scale print squares.

2. Place a 1½" purple square on a 2½" x 4½" small-scale print rectangle as shown. Sew on the drawn line, trim the seam allowance to ¼", and press. Make two. Repeat, placing the square on the opposite corner as shown.

Make 2.   Make 2.

3. Repeat with a 2" purple square on a 2½" small-scale print square. Make two.

Make 2.

4. Place a 2½" small-scale print square on the corner of the 4½" square of purple print. Stitch, trim, and press. Repeat with the two adjacent corners as shown. Make two.

Make 2.

5. Piece the Goblet blocks by sewing the units together as shown. Press.

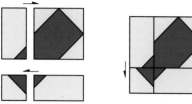

Make 2.

No-Mark Stitching
on the Diagonal

An Angler is a handy tool that is available at quilt shops. With it, you don't need to draw the diagonal stitching line.

6. Sew a triangle cut from the large-scale print on opposite sides of each Goblet block. Press toward the triangle and trim the sides even with the block.

7. Add the remaining triangles to opposite sides of the blocks from step 6. Trim each block to 11¾" square.

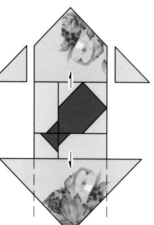

8. Sew the two Goblet blocks to each end of the 11¾" x 20½" large-scale print rectangle as shown in the quilt diagram.

9. Piece the three 1½" x 40" purple strips together and cut two strips, 1½" x 13¾", and two strips, 1½" x 43". Sew the 43"-long strips to the long sides of the runner. Press toward the purple. Sew the remaining strips to the two short sides of the runner. Press.

10. Sew the 4" x 43" strips of the medium-scale print to the long sides of the runner and press toward the outer border. Add the 4" x 20¾" strips to the short sides and press.

FINISHING

1. Refer to "Layering and Basting" on page 93 to prepare your table runner for quilting.

2. Quilt by hand or machine as desired.

3. Bind the table runner using the 2½" strips of medium-scale print, referring to "Binding" on page 94.

HOSTING A WINE-PAIRING PARTY

A wine-pairing event isn't just another cocktail party. Guests are seated and each person receives a small amount of wine and cheese. The wine and cheese are savored and evaluated, and then the next pairing is introduced. Lots of discussion is encouraged. Here are some tips in case you'd like to hold your own event.

*   Use clear glasses in order to see the clarity and color of the wine. Plastic glasses can be used, but because this is an event of some sophistication and elegance, I suggest borrowing, renting, or buying more glasses if you do not already have enough. The glasses can either be rinsed with water or replaced with clean glasses after each type of wine is introduced.

*   Provide ample water for guests. We give each person a bottle of commercially bottled water, but several carafes of water would work fine, too.

*   Cleanse the palate between pairings. Small slices of fresh pear are perfect as palate cleansers.

*   Some guests may be interested in taking home a list of the wines and cheeses they have sampled. Prepare a list and hand it out as a reminder of the special event. They can make notes on it as well.

Words of Wisdom

EVEN THOUGH THIS IS A SIMPLE QUILT, IT IS VERY PERSONAL. DURING THE WINE-AND-CHEESE PARTY, GUESTS CHOSE A PREPRINTED QUILT LABEL AND WROTE ADVICE TO THE COUPLE ON IT. THE BACKGROUND FABRICS WERE CHOSEN TO COORDINATE WITH THE COUPLE'S KITCHEN.

I NEEDED TO INCLUDE MORE LABELS THAN THERE WERE GUESTS TO MAKE THIS QUILT LARGE ENOUGH FOR MY INTENDED PURPOSE—TO USE AS A TABLECLOTH. WEDDING GUEST SIGNATURES WERE ADDED LATER, AS WELL AS SENTIMENTAL QUOTATIONS. (NO, MAYA ANGELOU AND ROBERT BURNS DID *NOT* ATTEND THE PARTY OR THE WEDDING!)

QUILT SIZE: 51½" x 58½"
BLOCK SIZE: 4¾" x 6¾"

MATERIALS

Yardage is based on 42"-wide fabric.

⅞ yard of fabric for outer border

⅓ yard of fabric for inner border

¼ yard *each* of 15 assorted fabrics for label backgrounds and binding

60 assorted quilt labels, 4¾" x 6¾" or smaller*

3½ yards of fabric for backing**

58" x 65" piece of very thin batting or prewashed cotton flannel

*Preprinted quilt labels are available by the yard at most quilt shops. I used labels from three different bolts so they would not be too coordinated.

**Use a tablecloth fabric for the backing if desired. See the photograph on page 45. You will need 2 yards of 60"-wide tablecloth fabric.

CUTTING

All measurements include ¼"-wide seam allowances.

From *each* of the 15 assorted fabrics, cut:
4 rectangles, 5¼" x 7¼" (60 total)
2½"-wide strips of varying lengths for binding

From the inner-border fabric, cut:
5 strips, 1¾" x 42"

From the outer-border fabric, cut:
6 strips, 4½" x 42"

INSTRUCTIONS

1. Cut apart your collection of quilt labels, trimming them so that each one measures 4¾" x 6¾", or smaller if necessary. Center each label on a 5¼" x 7¼" rectangle of assorted fabric, and topstitch in place using a zigzag or other decorative stitch.

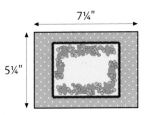

7¼"

5¼"

2. Arranging the prints and labels randomly, sew the rectangles in 10 rows of six rectangles each. Press the seams in opposite directions from row to row. Sew the rows together and press the seams in one direction.

3. Piece the five inner-border strips together end to end. Cut two strips, 1¾" x 41", and sew to the top and bottom edges of the quilt top. Cut two strips, 1¾" x 50½", and sew to the sides of the quilt top.

4. Piece the outer-border strips together end to end. Cut two strips, 4½" x 43½", and sew to the top and bottom edges of the quilt top. Cut two strips, 4½" x 58½", and sew to the sides of the quilt top.

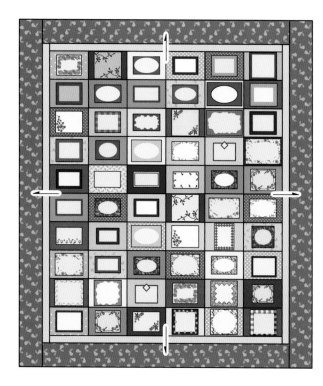

FINISHING

1. The quilt backing is actually yardage sold for tablecloths. The line drawings from the party (see opposite page) were taped on a large glass window with the cloth hanging over it. The light shining through enabled me to trace the images onto the backing using a permanent marker. For this project I used a marker with a fairly bold tip.

2. As another reminder of the event, you can create photo transfers of the wine labels using your favorite method. Perhaps the cheese will have labels you might use, too. I simply machine stitched them in place at the same time the backing was prepared.

3. Refer to "Layering and Basting" on page 93 to prepare your quilt for quilting.

4. Quilt by hand or machine as desired.

5. Using the 2½" strips cut from the 15 assorted fabrics, sew the strips together randomly end to end to form a piece approximately 6½ yards (232") long. Use this to bind the quilt, referring to "Binding" on page 94.

QUILT BACKING MADE OF TABLECLOTH YARDAGE

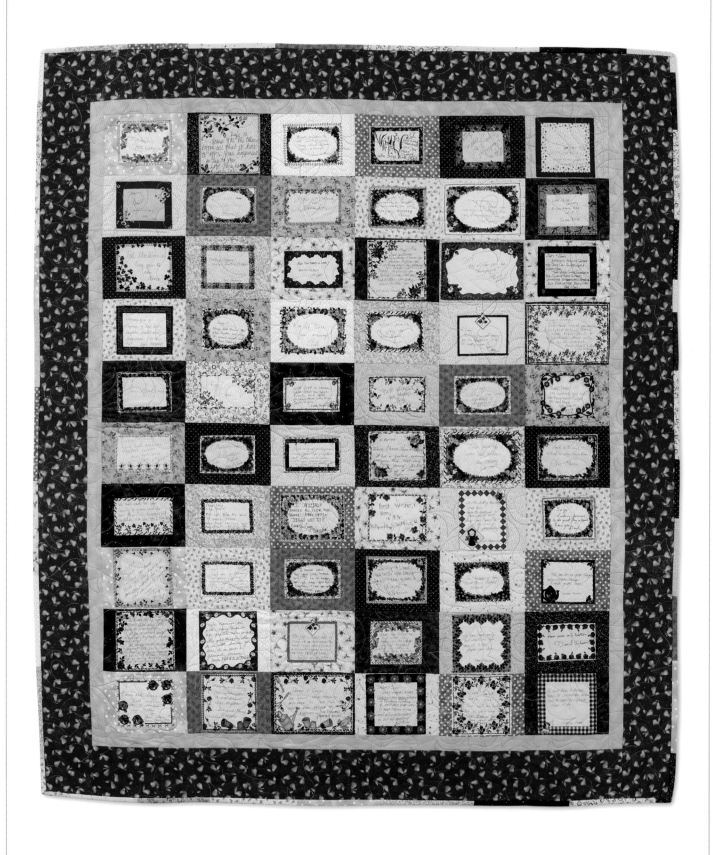

The following suggestions are tasty additions to a wine-and-cheese pairing. After the pairing, we offered several selections of soup and bread, along with an appropriate wine. For dessert we served poached pears, truffles, and a dessert wine.

- Danish Blue—A mellow blue flavor that is great for first timers. Pair with Pinot Blanc or Pinot Grigio.

- English Peppercorn—A mature Welsh cheddar blended with whole black peppercorns. Pair with Shiraz, Zinfandel, or Malbec.

- Supreme Brie—A French Brie that has a creamy, grassy flavor. Pair with Sauvignon Blanc.

- Smoked Gruyère—An American Gruyère with a smoky, nutty flavor. Pair with Cabernet Sauvignon.

- Smoked Mozzarella—An American semifirm cheese. Pair with Pinot Grigio or Riesling.

- Hot Pepper—A Monterey Jack cheese with peppers. Pair with Pinot Noir or Merlot.

- Mediterranean—A creamy Monterey Jack cheese with Mediterranean spices. Pair with Sauvignon Blanc.

Perfect Poached Pears

INGREDIENTS

5 cups water

¾ cup sugar

1 stick cinnamon

10 thin slices fresh ginger, peeled

3 pears (slightly underripe)

1 lemon

PREPARATION

1. Pound ginger slices with mallet until mashed.

2. Combine water, sugar, cinnamon stick, and ginger in a large pot. Heat until boiling. Simmer for 30 minutes.

3. Peel pears. Cut the lemon in half and rub the pears with lemon to prevent browning.

4. Squeeze the remaining juice from the lemon halves into the cinnamon-ginger liquid. Remove any seeds.

5. Add pears to cinnamon-ginger liquid. Heat until boiling and then simmer, uncovered, 25 to 30 minutes, or until the pears are just tender. Poke them with the tip of a knife to test them. If the knife slides in easily, they are done. Remove and place in a bowl.

6. Strain the liquid to remove ginger and cinnamon stick. Transfer 3 cups of the cooking liquid to a smaller sauce-pan. Heat liquid until boiling, reduce the heat. Cook about 35 minutes, or until the liquid thickens like syrup.

7. Arrange the pears in serving bowls and pour the cinnamon-ginger syrup over pears. Ice cream is a favorite addition.

Yield: 3 servings

AUTUMN HARVEST

Shhh, just listen to the sounds of the season. Sit on your porch and simply watch as the leaves spiral. Take a minute to ponder the brilliance of an autumn leaf.

I love the grandeur of autumn; it is a brief, but dramatic, season. It brings me peace and pleasure. Autumn just seems to fit my personality. I've always looked forward to the golden moments of fall. To me there is no season that is quite as captivating. I pause to give thanks and to reflect.

Some of my earliest memories are of autumn in rural Iowa. Unlike the corn and soybeans harvested on my childhood farm, our crop now consists of a few vegetables from the garden or farmer's market, but nonetheless, we take stock.

Celebrate autumn's arrival by throwing a harvest party. If you are inviting guests who do not know each other, a fun way to encourage them to get acquainted is by asking them to put five things in a brown paper bag that tell something about themselves—pictures of family, grandchildren, their favorite food, latest quilt, or one-of-a-kind items. At random, take the items from the bags and try to guess who brought what. It is amazing what we find out about each other.

Lessons are taught by the seasons. It's all about the ebb and flow. Spring makes a promise of things to come. Fall is the reward for the manual labors. It is indeed a spellbinding time of year.

LEAVES FROM A FALL WALK

CREATED BY MARGARET ZIEGLER

RING NEW DIMENSION TO YOUR QUILTS WITH LEAF PRINT-
ING. I ONCE READ THAT THE PATTERN OF A TREE'S BRANCHES
RESEMBLES THE VEINS IN ITS LEAVES. AS YOU COLLECT LEAVES, YOU CAN SEE
IF THAT HOLDS TRUE. AT ANY RATE, BOTH THE LEAF SHAPES AND THE VEINS
MAKE WONDERFUL DESIGNS FOR PRINTING ON FABRIC. YOU CAN ALSO TRY
OTHER FRUITS OR VEGETABLES FROM YOUR REFRIGERATOR OR GARDEN, SUCH
AS APPLES AND GREEN PEPPERS. RECENTLY I TRIED CELERY PRINTING. ONCE
YOU GET STARTED, YOU'LL BE AMAZED AT THE DESIGNS, AND I CAN PROMISE
THAT YOU WILL BE HOOKED ON PRINTING. YOU'LL ALSO BE AMAZED AT HOW
QUICKLY THIS TABLE RUNNER GOES TOGETHER—YOU WILL PIECE AND QUILT
THE BLOCKS AT THE SAME TIME.

TABLE RUNNER SIZE: 12½" x 42½"
BLOCK SIZE: 12" x 14"

MATERIALS

Yardage is based on 42"-wide fabric.

¼ yard of light fabric for block centers, washed and
   dried in preparation for printing

¼ yard of light print

¼ yard of medium-light print

¼ yard of medium-dark print

¼ yard of dark print

⅜ yard of fabric for binding

1 yard of fabric for backing

3 pieces of batting, 13" x 15½"

Acrylic paint in 3 to 4 colors and fabric extender*

1"-wide foam brush

*Jacquard paint works well; see "Resources" on
page 96. A fabric extender, available at craft stores,
makes the paint more permanent on fabric.*

CUTTING

All measurements include ¼"-wide seam allowances.

From the light fabric, cut:
3 rectangles, 4½" x 6½"

From the backing fabric, cut:
3 rectangles, 14" x 16½"
2 strips, 2" x 12½"

From the light print, cut:
4 strips, 1½" x 40"

From the medium-dark print, cut:
4 strips, 1½" x 40"

From the medium-light print, cut:
4 strips, 1½" x 40"

From the dark print, cut:
4 strips, 1½" x 40"

From the binding fabric, cut:
4 strips, 2" x 40"

LEAF PRINTING

1. Select leaves and stems for printing. Use flat, broad leaves. Ferns work well, and grasses and sagebrush give interesting results. Do not dry the leaves; they work better when flexible. Transport the leaves between the pages of a firm magazine or book. The same leaves can be used repeatedly.

2. Squirt a small amount of paint onto a paper plate. Add a dab of fabric extender to the paint and stir it around. Paint the underside of a flattened leaf using the foam brush. Do not coat the leaves too thickly with paint; the leaf's veins should be visible.

3. Place the leaf, paint side down, on the right side of a 4½" x 6½" rectangle of light fabric. Cover the painted leaf with a paper towel. Roll over the leaf several times with a roller, a plastic paint bottle, or the palm of your hand. Lift the leaf gently from the tip, pulling straight up. If you want the stems a different color, print the leaves first, then the stems.

4. Print a second color after the first color has been applied. The paint dries very quickly and I don't mind if it blends a bit. I also leave the original color of paint on the paper plate and blend in the new color with the brush.

5. Let the paint dry completely and then heat-set with an iron according to the paint manufacturer's instructions.

MAKING THE LOG CABIN BLOCKS

You will be constructing two blocks using the light print and medium-dark strips in the first position around the center. You will construct one block using the medium print and dark print strips in the first position around the center. On one side of the block you will alternate the light print with the medium-light print as the rows progress from the center to the outside of the block. On the other side of the block you will alternate the medium-dark print with the dark print as the rows progress from the center to the outside of the block.

1. Lay a 14" x 16½" backing rectangle on a flat surface with the wrong side facing up. Center a 13" x 15½" piece of quilt batting on top of the backing rectangle. Center a 4½" x 6½" leaf-printed rectangle right side up on top of the batting rectangle. Pin in place.

2. With right sides together and edges matching, place a 1½" strip on one of the 4½" sides of the center rectangle. Leave a tail of about ½" at the beginning. Pin to hold in place. Sew a ¼" seam along the edges of the center rectangle. Finger-press the seam open and pin.

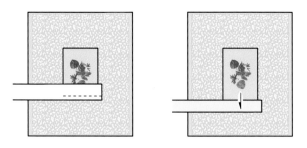

3. Sew another 1½" strip of the same print to your block in the same manner, moving clockwise around the center piece. Trim the tail from the first strip. Finger-press the seam open. Pin to hold it in place.

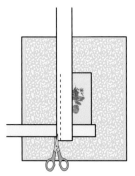

4. Continue working clockwise around the block, switching fabrics when necessary, until you have four rows of logs on each side of the beginning center rectangle. Trim away the excess batting and backing. The block should measure 12½" x 14½".

Make 2.

Make 1.

JOINING THE BLOCKS

Refer to the quilt photo at right for the layout design.

1. Fold the two 2" x 12½" joining fabric strips (cut from the backing fabric) in half lengthwise, wrong sides together, and press.

2. Starting at one end of the quilt, join two blocks by pinning them right sides together on the short side, along with one of the folded joining strips and stitching through all the layers. Add the third block in the same manner. Press the seams open. Press the joining strips over on the back to cover the seam allowance, and hand sew in place.

3. Since the runner was quilted as it was sewn, just bind it using the 2" strips, referring to "Binding" on page 94. It's ready to use!

RING OF LEAVES
IN THEIR SHOUTING COLORS

CREATED BY JANE QUINN. QUILTED BY DEB BARTH.

TAKE A MINUTE TO PONDER THE BRILLIANCE OF AN AUTUMN LEAF. COLLECT SEVERAL AND USE THEM AS PATTERNS FOR FUSIBLE APPLI-QUÉ ON THIS DOUBLE WEDDING RING TABLE RUNNER. YOU'LL HAVE FUN TAKING WALKS TO LOOK FOR INTERESTING LEAVES, JUST AS MOST OF US DID AS CHILDREN. YOU'LL HAVE FUN MAKING THIS QUILT, TOO—THE EASY WAY WITH NO CURVED PIECING!

TABLE RUNNER SIZE: 23" x 57½"

MATERIALS

Yardage is based on 42"-wide fabric.

1⅛ yards of light print for inner background

1 yard of medium green print for outer background

¼ yard *each* of 6 assorted prints for rings

¼ yard *each* of 2 prints for jewels

½ yard of fabric for binding

1⅞ yards of fabric for backing

29" x 62" piece of batting

Template plastic or Double Wedding Ring pieced arc template from Quiltsmart

3 panels of Double Wedding Ring fusible interfacing from Quiltsmart

Fusible web

CUTTING

All measurements include ¼"-wide seam allowances.

From *each* of the 6 ring fabrics, cut:
2 strips, 3" x 40" (12 total)

From the light print, cut:
4 squares, 12" x 12"

10 rectangles, 3" x 12"

From *each* of the 2 jewel fabrics, cut:
2 strips, 2½" x 40" (4 total); cut into 18 squares, 2½" x 2½"

From the medium green print, cut:
10 rectangles, 6" x 12"

4 squares, 6" x 6"

From the binding fabric, cut:
5 strips, 2½" x 40"

INSTRUCTIONS

The quilt shown was made using Double Wedding Ring printed fusible interfacing from Quiltsmart. With this method, you assemble the patchwork arcs with straight seams, stitch them to the interfacing, and then fuse the pieced arcs to a large background square. Use your sewing machine to zigzag stitch the edges in place, and you're done! This product makes fast and easy work of a Double Wedding Ring quilt.

Look for Quiltsmart at your local quilt shop, or see "Resources" on page 96. You can purchase the interfacing in bulk, packaged with a book, or by individual panels. For this project you need just three panels, and the small expense is well worth the time savings and ease of piecing.

SWEET SUGAR COOKIE MEMORIES

The first Christmas after I opened my shop, Quilting in the Country, I wanted to thank my loyal customers and friends for their support. The gift I decided on that first year was an inspiring demonstration by an interior designer. She presented simple holiday decorating hints and discussed age-old traditions. Everyone brought cookies and copies of their recipes to share. There wasn't any particular rule as to the number of cookies to bring. Bring some, eat some, and take some home! That was the beginning of our tradition.

Now each year, a group of special women friends gather for Quilting in the Country's Annual Holiday Cookie Exchange to enjoy holiday concoctions and lighthearted banter. It's an event I love and would never consider canceling, no matter how hectic the holiday season becomes!

We gather together on a Saturday afternoon in early December not just to share goodies, but to relax before the hustle and bustle of the holiday season really gets rolling. This date also encourages me to get an early start on holiday decorating and baking.

The projects in the section are easy to make and fun to use for your own cookie exchange or any type of Christmas gathering. I've even included a few favorite cookie and beverage recipes, as well as tips on hosting a cookie exchange to help you begin your own tradition.

WARM UP WITH WINTER FRIENDS

A winter picnic may be just the cure for cabin fever. We all get hungry for a change, even if we've been spending time involved in winter outdoor activities.

By the time you've put away all your holiday decorations (even the Valentines), if you're like me you're anxiously awaiting spring. But it just never seems to come. That's when I like to hold an end-of-winter picnic.

Invite friends to arrive after a day of skiing or snowshoeing. Our most memorable winter picnics have included an evening of moonlight cross-country skiing or sledding. If you have the space and wood to burn, start a bonfire outdoors for the returning skiers. By celebrating winter this way, I almost feel as though I'm defying it!

Simply getting ready for the winter party helps chase off the winter blahs. The picnic food is so welcome after an outing in the snowy fields. Use the tablecloths you would usually use in the summertime. Find the paper plates and plastic forks and spoons. Buy some fresh flowers in cheerful summer colors of red, yellow, orange, and spring green. And don't forget to display all your bright and cheery quilts—the ones you usually reserve for summer. Decorate the entire house with them. I like to spread them on the floor in front of the fireplace and encourage picnic guests to sit on them. The bugs won't bother them at this picnic!

backing with tape or heavy pins, depending on whether your surface is hard or soft. Center the batting on top of the backing, and then center the quilt top with right side up on the batting. Smooth out the quilt top so that all the seam allowances are facing the proper direction. Use safety pins across the whole surface of the quilt to hold the layers together for machine quilting. A good spacing rule is to have one pin every 6". For hand quilting, use thread basting in a grid of about 6". Remove the anchor pins or tape from the outer edge of the backing.

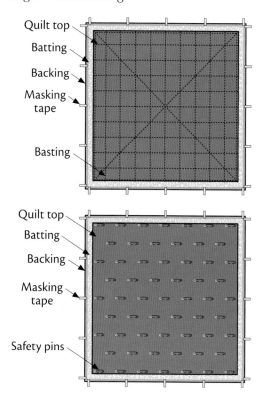

QUILTING

Quilt by hand or machine. For more details on machine quilting, refer to *Machine Quilting Made Easy!* by Maurine Noble (Martingale & Company, 1994). For hand quilting, see *Loving Stitches*, revised edition, by Jeana Kimball (Martingale & Company, 2003).

TYING

Tying a quilt is another way to hold the layers together. I like it because it's quick and the ties add a decorative element to the quilt. You can use embroidery floss, pearl cotton, or thin yarn for

tying. You can even incorporate buttons into the ties as I did in "Wool Mitten Friends" on page 82.

Ties are basically square knots and can be made one at a time or sequentially without cutting the thread in between each time. Use a sturdy sharp needle with an eye large enough for the thread you are using. Insert the needle through all layers of the quilt and bring it back up again. Make the knots every 3" to 4" apart unless directed otherwise in the project instructions.

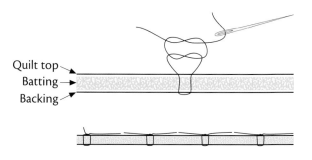

BINDING

After quilting your project, you are ready to add the binding. The width of the strips can vary from 2" to 3½", depending on how narrow or wide you want your binding to appear. A standard width is 2½", but if you are working with flannels you may want to cut your strips 3" or 3½" wide to accommodate the extra fluffiness of the fabrics. If your project is small with fine detail, you may want to cut your binding strips 2" wide. If your quilt has curved edges, cut your binding strips on the bias of the fabric so that your binding has more stretch.

Once you have enough strips cut to go around all sides of your quilt with an extra 8" to 10", you are ready to join the strips end to end into one continuous piece. Join the strips at a 45° angle as shown to reduce the bulk. Press the seams open.

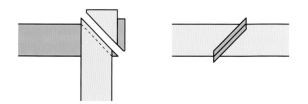

1. Press the strips in half lengthwise with the wrong sides together. Cut the beginning end of the binding at a 45° angle, and press under

½" along the end. Pin this end on one side of the quilt top with the raw edges of the binding lined up with the edge of the quilt top. Begin stitching about 6" from the beginning of the binding, using a ¼" seam allowance, and stop ¼" from the corner of the quilt. Backstitch and cut the threads.

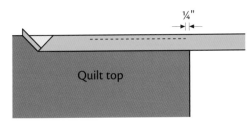

2. Turn the quilt so that you will be able to stitch the next edge of the quilt. Fold the binding up and away from the quilt so that the raw edges of the binding are in line with the next edge of the quilt. The fold just formed in the binding will make a 45° angle pointing in from the corner of the quilt.

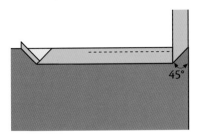

3. Using your finger to hold the 45° fold in place, fold the binding back down over the quilt top so that the raw edges of the binding are lined up with the quilt where they will be stitched. The newly formed fold of the binding will be even with the previously stitched edge of the quilt. Still using a ¼" seam allowance, begin stitching ¼" from the edge of the quilt and stitch along the side of the quilt, stopping ¼" before the next corner.

4. Repeat steps 2 and 3 for each side of the quilt. When you get close to the beginning of the binding that is pinned in place, cut the end of the binding so that there will be enough to tuck 1" inside the opening formed in the beginning. Continue stitching over the joining area, overlapping your beginning line of stitching.

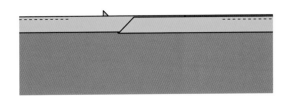

5. Trim the edges of the backing and batting so that they are even with the quilt top unless instructed otherwise. Fold the binding over to the back so that the fold just covers the line of stitching that holds the binding. Use an appliqué stitch to sew the binding to the back of the quilt, mitering the corners with a fold.

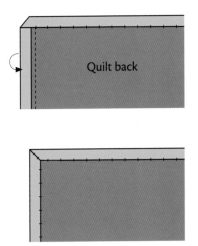

ADD A LABEL

Be sure to add a label to your quilt, including your name, the date, and place where the quilt was made. Add any other information you like, including a sentiment or quotation if the quilt will be a gift for a special occasion. If possible or appropriate, consider adding a photo image to the label using photo-transfer paper or other methods.

RESOURCES

Jacquard
www.jacquardproducts.com
Paint-Color for Quilters

Quilting in the Country
5100 S. 19th Rd.
Bozeman, MT 59718
406-587-8216
www.QuiltingInTheCountry.com

Sweet pea poster-print fabric, miniature vintage kitchen ornaments, vintage reproduction tablecloth

Quiltsmart
7801 Park Dr. Ste. E
Chanhassen, MN 55317
888-446-5750
www.quiltsmart.com

Double Wedding Ring printed interfacing and pattern booklet, Drunkard's Path printed interfacing and pattern booklet, 2" On Point Gridded Interfacing

Wimpole Street
800-765-0504

Tiny knitted long johns, sweaters, and mittens

ABOUT THE AUTHOR

Jane Quinn started Quilting in the Country in 1991, fulfilling a lifelong dream to have her own cozy quilt shop where she could give personal attention to every quilt project. At first, Jane offered quilt classes in her home, a two-story farmhouse located three miles outside of Bozeman, Montana, but soon she began selling quilt fabric and the books required for her classes. In the summer of 1996, no longer able to contain the business inside their home, Jane and Bill Quinn renovated the bunkhouse on their century-old farmstead, and the next era of Quilting in the Country began.

In 1998, Quilting in the Country received national recognition as one of the 10 best quilt shops in America. Jane's annual outdoor quilt show, drawing approximately 5,000 visitors from near and far, is a visual and creative treat for those who love to quilt, as well as those who simply appreciate stunning artwork displayed in a beautiful setting.

Jane has designed many of her own unique quilt patterns. She has written a book on hosting quilt retreats, and she has also authored four of her own cookbooks: *Soup's On, Salad Sampler, Daily Desserts,* and *Cookies to Share with Family and Friends.* You are sure to find just the right recipe to warm your heart and soul, and maybe connect with a time gone by, through one of Jane's books.

Jane lives with her husband, Bill, as well as three cats, five ducks, and assorted sheep in Bozeman, Montana.

People will forget what you said;
People will forget what you did;
But people will never forget how you made them feel.

—A. Altamiro